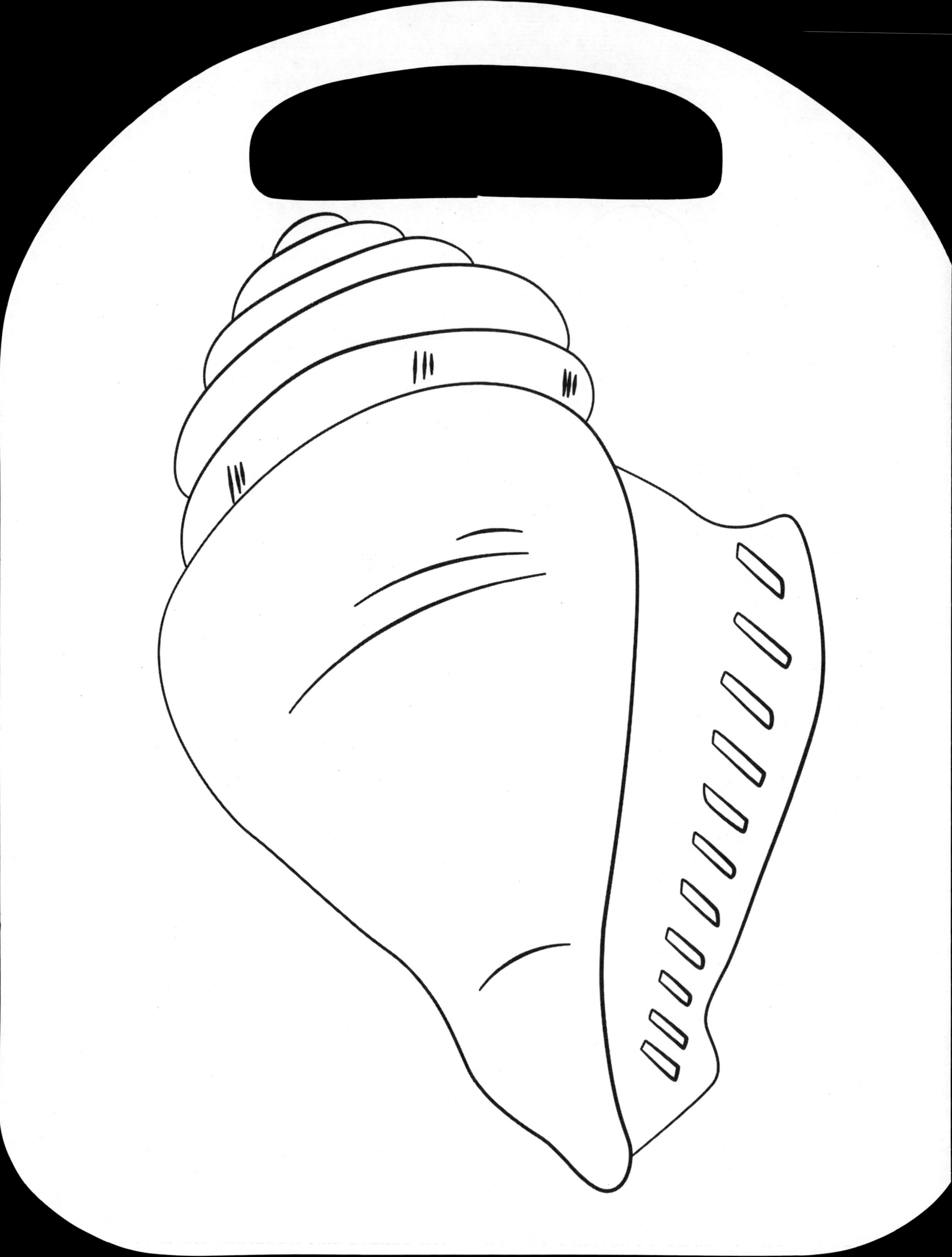

Pages and pages of creatures from the sea to colour! Get this handy, bag-shaped colouring book for your little one. This easy-to-carry book with cute, black-and-white illustrations to colour is the perfect companion for every preschooler.

- **Will keep children occupied for hours**
- **Fun way for children to learn about colours and colouring**
- **Ideal book to improve children's motor skills and encourage creativity**

COLOURMANIA

Scan Now!

Children | Colouring US$ 4.95

978-81-319-3747-1

PEGASUS

www.pegasusforkids.com

₹90

001

9788131937471